Encounters with God

The Epistle of Paul
the Apostle to the
PHILIPPIANS

Encounters with God Study Guide Series

Encounters with God

The Epistle of Paul the Apostle to the PHILIPPIANS

Published by Thomas Nelson, Inc., P.O. Box 141000, Nashville, Tennessee 37214.

Scripture quotations are taken from The New King James Version® (NKJV), copyright 1979, 1980, 1982, 1992 Thomas Nelson, Inc., Publishers.

Library of Congress Cataloging-in-Publication Data
ISBN 1-4185-26487

Printed in the United States of America

08 09 10 11 RRD 9 8 7 6 5 4 3 2 1

All Scripture references are from the New King James Version of the Bible.

CONTENTS

AN INTRODUCTION TO THE EPISTLE OF PHILIPPIANS

The Book of Philippians is an "epistle"—a formal letter intended to give instruction. The letter was written by the apostle Paul to the believers in the Greek city of Philippi while Paul was in prison (1:13,14), almost certainly in Rome (Acts 28:16–31), in 61–62 AD. Paul may have been confined, but he had not been prevented from communicating with churches and preaching the gospel to his captors (Philippians 1:14–14).

Paul had no doubt that the church in Philippi was the result of a divine encounter. On his second missionary journey, Paul had experienced a vision calling him to preach the gospel in Macedonia. Philippi was his next stop!

The original name of Philippi was Krenides, meaning "little fountains." The town was in a beautiful natural setting, on a hill with an abundance of springs for water supply. The city was later renamed for Philip II of Macedon, the father of Alexander the Great. It was a strategic trade center located on the Egnatian Way, which connected the eastern provinces of the Roman Empire to Rome. A famous battle was fought at Philippi—Cassius and Brutus, Julius Caesar's assassins, fought Octavius and Mark Antony, with the latter duo victorious. In the aftermath of the battle, Philippi was classified as a Roman colony in 42 BC, making its people Roman citizens with the right to purchase or sell property. Octavius declared himself to be Caesar and changed his name to Augustus. He was emperor at the time of Jesus' birth.

In Paul's day nearly a century later, the Philippians continued to enjoy special legal status, and had privileges in civil courts and exemption from paying poll and land taxes. This produced tremendous wealth and status, which also led to pride and attitudes of superiority.

In Philippi, Paul met Lydia and other women meeting for prayer along a river bank (Acts 16:13). A church was established in Lydia's home and like the city as a whole, the church at Philippi had a blended congregation from its outset. The church members likely included Lydia, an upper-class woman who sold expensive purple dye; a slave girl formerly possessed by an evil spirit (Acts 16:16–18); a middle-class jailer (Acts 16:25–34); and a mix of Gentile races and cultures, along with a small but influential group of Jews.

Paul gave specific instruction to the Philippians about how to pray, how to live above anxiety, how to believe, how to think, and how to behave. His message was to mature believers as well as to those who were being added to the church. He encouraged the church to remain joyful in the face of persecution, continue to be humble in service, and walk steadfastly in faith.

This church was dear to Paul's heart and his message to it is filled with joy. He addressed several in the church by name. He sought to encourage the Philippian believers as his partners in ministry, and to commend the work of Timothy and Epaphroditus. Paul reported the ways in which God had worked and continued to minister in his life. His joy was not based on his circumstance, but rather, on his relationship with Christ Jesus. Throughout, the letter is very personal and overflowing with thanksgiving and benediction.

About the Author, the Apostle Paul. The author of this book was the apostle Paul, writing from a Roman prison in approximately 60-63 AD.

Paul's name was originally Saul (Acts 13:9), the royal name of Israel's first king. Upon his conversion, he adopted the name Paul, which literally meant "little" and reflected his self-evaluation as being "the least of the apostles" (1 Corinthians 15:98). Certainly in the history of Christianity, the "little" apostle became the foremost apostle to the Gentile world.

Paul was a Roman citizen, his hometown being Tarsus, the chief city of Cilicia. He was fluent in Greek, studied philosophy and theology under Gamaliel, and was also a Hebrew, the son of a Pharisee from the tribe of Benjamin. Paul, too, became a Pharisee, an extremely strict follower of Jewish religious laws. By trade, he was a tentmaker. This unique blend of cultural, religious, and experiential factors gave Paul unusual entrée into both Gentile and Jewish circles. This was especially important in an international trade center such as Ephesus.

Initially, Paul was a major force in denouncing Christianity in Jerusalem, and had enthusiastically supported Stephen's martyrdom. While on a mission to seek out and destroy Christians who had traveled to Syria, Paul had a dramatic encounter with the risen Christ and became as zealous a believer in Christ Jesus and advocate for the Gospel as he once had been a determined foe to the early church. He took several fruitful and demanding missionary journeys, spending as long as two years in some areas to teach those who had heeded the Gospel message and accepted Jesus as their Savior. Over the decades of his ministry, he became the most influential church planter and theologian in the early church. His letters addressed both the triumphs and difficulties encountered by the first-century Christians, many of whom faced intense persecution for their faith.

The issues that Paul addressed in his letters to the first-century church are no less important to today's believers. Paul laid a practical foundation for *how* to live the Christian life, even in the face of struggles, temptations, and heresies. His personal example of seeking to know and obey Christ Jesus no matter what the cost, remains an example to all who call themselves Christians. "I in Christ and Christ in me" was Paul's unwavering theme song.

AN OVERVIEW OF OUR STUDY
OF THE EPISTLE OF PHILIPPIANS

This study guide presents seven lessons drawn from and based largely upon the Epistle of Philippians. The study guide elaborates upon, and is based upon, the commentary included in the *Blackaby Study Bible:*

Lesson #1: Joy That Christ Is Preached

Lesson #2: Unity through Humility

Lesson #3: Staying on Course

Lesson #4: Pressing toward the High Goal

Lesson #5: Rising above Anxiety

Lesson #6: The Godly Thought Life

Lesson #7: The Key to Confidence

Personal or Group Use. These lessons are offered for personal study and reflection, or for small-group Bible study. The questions asked may be answered by an individual reader, or used as a foundation for group discussion. A segment titled "Notes to Leaders of Small Groups" is included at the back of this book to help those who might lead a group study of the material here.

Before you embark on this study, we encourage you to read in full the statement in the Blackaby Study Bible titled "How to Study the Bible." Our contention is always that the Bible is unique among all literature. It is God's definitive word for humanity. The Bible is:

- *inspired*—"God breathed"

- *authoritative*—absolutely the "final word" on any spiritual matter

- *the plumb line of truth*—the standard against which all human activity and reasoning must be evaluated

The Bible is fascinating in that it has remarkable diversity, but also remarkable unity. The books were penned by a diverse assortment of authors representing a variety of languages and cultures. The Bible as a whole has a number of literary forms. But, the Bible's message from cover to cover is clear, consistent, and unified.

More than mere words on a page, the Bible is an encounter with God Himself. No book is more critical to your life. The very essence of the Bible is the Lord Himself.

God speaks by the Holy Spirit through the Bible. He also communicates during your time of prayer, in your life circumstances, and through the church. Read your Bible in an attitude of prayer, and allow the Holy Spirit to make you aware of God's activity in your personal life. Write down what you learn, meditate on it, and adjust your thoughts, attitudes, and behavior accordingly. Look for ways every day in which the truth of God's Word can be applied to your circumstances and relationships. God is not random, but orderly and intentional in the way He speaks to you.

Be encouraged—the Bible is *not* too difficult for the average person to understand if that person asks the Holy Spirit for help. (Furthermore, not even the most brilliant person can fully understand the Bible apart from the Holy Spirit's assistance!) God desires for you to know Him and to understand His Word. Every person who reads the Bible can learn from it. The person who will receive *maximum* benefit from reading and studying the Bible, however, is the one who:

- *is born again* (John 3:3, 5). Those who are born again and have received the gift of His Spirit have a distinct advantage in understanding the deeper truths of God's Word.

- *has a heart that desires to learn God's truth.* Your attitude influences greatly the outcome of your Bible study. Resist the temptation to focus on what others have said about the Bible. Allow the Holy Spirit to guide you as you study God's Word for yourself.

- *has a heart that seeks to obey God.* The Holy Spirit teaches those who desire to apply what they learn.

Begin your Bible study with prayer, asking the Holy Spirit to guide your thoughts and to impress upon you what is on God's heart. Then, make plans to adjust your life immediately to obey the Lord fully.

As you read and study the Bible, your purpose is not to *create* meaning, but to *discover* the truth of the text with the Holy Spirit's guidance. Ask yourself, "What did the author have in mind? How was this applied by those who first heard these words?" Especially in your study of the Gospel accounts, pay attention to the words of Jesus that begin "truly, truly" or "He opened His mouth and taught them saying." These are core principles and teachings that have powerful impact on *every* person's life.

At times you may find it helpful to consult other passages of the Bible (made available in the center columns in the Blackaby Study Bible), or the commentary that is in the margins of the Blackaby Study Bible.

Always keep in mind that Bible study is not primarily an exercise for acquiring information, but an opportunity for transformation. Bible study is your opportunity to encounter God and to be changed in His presence. When God speaks to your heart, nothing remains the same. Jesus said, "He who has ears to hear, let him hear" (Matt. 13:9). Choose to have ears that desire to hear!

The B-A-S-I-Cs of Each Study in This Guide. Each lesson in this study guide has five segments, using the word BASIC as an acronym. The word BASIC does not allude to elementary or "simple," but rather, to "foundational." These studies extend the concepts that are part of the Blackaby Study Bible commentary and are focused on key aspects of what it means to be a Christ-follower in today's world. The BASIC acronym stands for:

B = *Bible Focus.* This segment presents the central passage for the lesson and a general explanation that covers the central theme or concern.

A = *Application for Today.* This segment has a story or illustration related to modern-day times, with questions that link the Bible text to today's issues, problems, and concerns.

S = *Supplementary Scriptures to Consider.* In this segment, other Bible verses related to the general theme of the lesson are explored.

I = *Introspection and Implications.* In this segment, questions are asked that lead to deeper reflection about one's personal faith journey and life experiences.

C = *Communicating the Good News.* In this segment, challenging questions are aimed at ways in which the truth of the lesson might be lived out and shared with others (either to win those who are unbelievers or to build up members of the church).

LESSON #1

JOY THAT CHRIST IS PREACHED

*Joy: an inner exuberance and vibrancy not
dependent upon external factors*

B
Bible Focus

> *But I want you to know, brethren, that the things which*
> *happened to me have actually turned out for the furtherance*
> *of the gospel, so that it has become evident to the whole*
> *palace guard, and to all the rest, that my chains are in Christ;*
> *and most of the brethren in the Lord, having become confident*
> *by my chains, are much more bold to speak the word without*
> *fear.*
>
> *Some indeed preach Christ even from envy and strife, and*
> *some also from goodwill: The former preach Christ from*
> *selfish ambition, not sincerely, supposing to add affliction to*
> *my chains; but the latter out of love, knowing that I am*
> *appointed for the defense of the gospel. What then? Only that*
> *in every way, whether in pretense or in truth, Christ is*
> *preached; and in this I rejoice, yes, and will rejoice*
> *(Philippians 1:12–18).*

Paul focused on results!

He longed to see Christ preached, regardless of a speaker's motives. Paul knew that the Word of God had power to convict, convince, and correct *regardless* of a speaker's attitudes or intentions.

We are often critical of those who seem to preach with insincerity or with motives of envy, strife, or self-ambition. Certainly it is far better for those who preach the Word to speak from goodwill, love, and truth. Either way, however, the Word has power of its own that transcends the vessel that delivers it. Consider a beautiful and highly valuable gift put in a tattered box and wrapped in torn and dirty paper. The value of the gift is nonetheless precious! So it is with God's Word. We must never lose sight of God's promise through the prophet Isaiah 55:10–11:

> For a the rain comes down, and the snow from heaven,
> And do not return there,
> But water the earth,
> And make it bring forth and bud,
> That it may give seed to the sower
> And bread to the eater,
> So shall My word be that goes forth from My mouth;
> It shall not return to Me void,
> But it shall accomplish what I please,
> And it shall prosper in the thing for which I sent it."

The comfort in this word from God is that we can trust God to use what we say that is in line with the truth of His Word, even if we are not the most skilled speaker and even if we feel unworthy or inadequate. God will be faithful to His own Word. We can also take comfort in knowing that it is *possible* to look beyond the messenger and rejoice that the MESSAGE is going forth. We need to take joy that God is using even those we might consider to be "unlikely and suspect candidates" to speak His Word to those who do not know it.

Does this give us license to live any way we want as long as we speak or preach an accurate message from God's Word? Not at all!

People do have a right to judge the way we live. Our behavior and speech reflects our attitudes, beliefs, and character. Our visible lives give a strong witness about Christ Jesus in us . . . or a very weak witness. When our words about the Word line up with our actions as a believer, we actually bear a *two-fold* witness to the world. The Word that we speak is one form of witness. The lives that are in line with God's word are a second witness.

There is great authority attached to a two-fold witness in Judaism and in Christianity. It is the way that the "truth" of a matter is established. Paul wrote to the Corinthians these words originally stated in the Book of Deuteronomy: "By the mouth of two or three witnesses every word shall be established" (2 Corinthians 13:1, Deuteronomy 19:15). Jesus said to His disciples, "The words that I speak to you I do not speak on My own author-ity; but the Father who dwells in Me does the works. Believe Me that I am in the Father and the Father in Me, or else believe Me for the sake of the works themselves" (John 14:10–11). In other words, Jesus was saying, "Believe in what I say, or believe in what I do. Either way, believe!"

When we act with integrity—our beliefs and attitudes lining up with our speech and behavior—our lives are a *full* reflection of the love and power of God at work in our world today. A truth is *established* in a way that is more powerful than either our verbal witness or character witness alone. Integrity of speech and behavior in presenting the Gospel is the goal to which we all should aspire, not just the preacher in the pulpit!

When we speak with integrity, *we* have strength and are established firmly in God's truth.

When we speak with integrity, *others* are affected more powerfully and are confronted with truth that cannot be denied.

A
Application for Today

"It backfired," the pastor of a church said with a tremendous sigh as he sat in a café booth across from a fellow pastor.

"What backfired?" the other pastor asked.

"The remodeling campaign at our church."

"How so?"

"Well," the first pastor explained, "we had a number of things that we wanted to do to beautify our church—especially the main sanctuary, the entrance to the church, and the hall that we use for social gatherings. We also wanted to beautify the back entrance just off the parking lot."

"I was with you in your church when that work was about half finished," the second pastor noted. "I thought things were on their way to looking splendid."

"They were," the first pastor said. "But as part of our campaign we told those who gave that we would be honoring their giving by putting their names on various plaques, of varying size."

"That's fairly common," the second pastor noted.

"Yes," said the first pastor, "but now we have a beautiful facility that is cluttered by *ugly plaques*!"

Paul didn't care who preached the Word. He gave God the credit! He acknowledged that the Gospel was what mattered most, not the individual who preached it.

Are you willing to give generously to your church *without* receiving any recognition for your giving?

How much are you willing to volunteer your time and talents without any recognition or note of appreciation?

Why do we seem to care so much about who gets the credit for good deeds?

S
Supplementary Scriptures to Consider

The apostle Paul maintained a joyful perspective even in prison:

> I know that this will turn out for my deliverance through your prayer and the supply of the Spirit of Jesus Christ, according to my earnest expectation and hope that in nothing I shall be ashamed, but with all boldness, as always, so now also Christ will be magnified in my body, whether by life or by death.
> For to me to live is Christ, and to die is gain
> (Philippians 2:19–21).

- Note that Paul asked that the Philippians pray that he would be a faithful witness ("in nothing . . . ashamed") and a bold witness. How do you respond to the challenge to be a faithful and bold witness?

- What does this phrase mean to you: "Christ will be magnified in my body, whether by life or by death"?

Paul also saw benefit for others in his suffering:

> If I am being poured out as a drink offering on the sacrifice
> and service of your faith, I am glad and rejoice with you all.
> For the same reason you also be glad and rejoice with me
> (Philippians 2:17–18).

- Drink offerings in the Old Testament were poured out over an altar as a symbol that the person's life was being made totally available to God. Paul regarded the sacrifice and service of the Philippians as a sign that his life had been poured out as an acceptable offering to God. Have you poured out your life in service to someone who is presently living for the

Lord? Do you see *their* life in Christ as a sign to *you* that God is pleased with the way you sacrificed on their behalf? To whom is your life being "poured out" in service?

Paul wrote in a similar vein to the Colossians:

> I now rejoice in my sufferings for you, and fill up in my flesh what is lacking in the afflictions of Christ, for the sake of His body, which is the church. . . . Him we preach, warning every man and teaching every man in all wisdom, that we may present every man perfect in Christ Jesus. To this end I also labor, striving according to His working which works in me mightily (Colossians 1:24, 28–29).

• To what degree do you feel responsible that others might see your life and hear your words in a way that causes them to mature spiritually in Christ Jesus? How does having such a perspective change your own speech and behavior? How does it give purpose and meaning to your life?

Paul held in high regard his colleagues who had suffered for the Gospel and remained true to their Savior and Lord:

> Therefore I sent him [Epaphroditus] the more eagerly, that when you see him again you may rejoice, and I may be less sorrowful. Receive him therefore in the Lord with all gladness,

and hold such men in esteem; because for the work of Christ
he came close to death, not regarding his life, to
supply what was lacking in your service toward me
(Philippians 2:28–30).

- Whom do you hold in esteem? Why?

I
Introspection and Implications

1. How difficult is it to identify one's own motives?

2. To what degree do you believe that your life has integrity—a full align-
ment of what you believe and think with how you speak and act? In
what ways might you live with greater integrity?

3. How important is integrity to a person's Christian witness?

4. What are you willing to do for the Gospel *even if nobody else knows* the full extent of what you do?

5. In what ways do you struggle with "rejoicing" that the Gospel is accurately preached by someone whom you dislike or mistrust personally?

C
Communicating the Good News

What responsibility do you have for the way others think or feel about Christ Jesus?

How do you believe *your* "inner motives" might be perceived by someone who hears you witness about Christ? Is this an accurate perception? Why or why not? If it is an inaccurate perception, what might you do? Do you feel God leading you to change your motives, and if so, how might you go about that?

LESSON #2

UNITY THROUGH HUMILITY

Humility: a total yielding to God that
results in being respectful of others, even
to the point of giving to others first

B
Bible Focus

> *Let your conduct be worthy of the gospel of Christ, so that whether I come and see you or am absent, I may hear of your affairs, that you stand fast in one spirit, with one mind striving together for the faith of the gospel, and not in any way terrified by your adversaries, which is to them a proof of perdition, but to you of salvation, and that from God. For to you it has been granted on behalf of Christ, not only to believe in Him, but also to suffer for His sake, having the same conflict which you saw in me and now hear is in me.*
>
> *Therefore if there is any consolation in Christ, if any comfort of love, if any fellowship of the Spirit, if any affection and mercy, fulfill my joy by being like-minded, having the same love, being of one accord, of one mind. Let nothing be done through selfish ambition or conceit, but in lowliness of mind let each esteem others better than himself. Let each of you look out not only for his own interests, but also for the interests of others (Philippians 1:27–2:4).*

We do not succeed alone. Everything that we know we learned from someone else—either directly from our relationship with that person or through their writings and other forms of communication. Everything that we have accomplished we have done because someone gave us opportunity, access, or assistance. Everything that we have earned we have earned because somebody else bought what we had to sell—whether product, services, time, energy, or some combination of all four.

Elsewhere in his epistle to the Philippians, the apostle Paul called upon the believers to recognize that they had not come to full reconciliation with God on their own efforts or goodness. They had been taught the Gospel and in the end, it was Christ who had secured their salvation. Each member of the church at Philippi was indebted to someone for having shared the Gospel with him, and ultimately, all of the believers were indebted to Christ Jesus for His sacrifice on the cross.

Because we do not succeed alone, Paul called upon the Philippians and all believers to look out for the interests of others. We are to see others as God views them and do whatever we can to meet their needs, even to putting them "first."

In this passage, Paul noted three things about the conduct that he desired to see in the Philippian believers:

First, he wanted them to stand fast in one spirit—having one mind and being of one accord in God's love. This unity of mind and heart, Paul wrote, would come as they embraced the same Gospel and were willing to face persecution together. Just as Father, Son, and Holy Spirit are united, those in the church are to be unified.

Second, he wanted them each to "esteem others better than himself." Paul defined in a few words the essence of humility—a total yielding of self to God, which allows God to empower a person both to serve others and to submit to them. Paul wrote that believers were to have "lowliness of mind." This does not have anything to do with intelligence, but rather, humility. Humility is trading in our "I'm number one" perspective for an ability to see the needs in other people. Just as Christ served others rather than Himself, even to death on the cross, we are to serve others.

Third, he wanted them to live without fear of their enemies. The word "perdition" refers to ruin or destruction. Paul said that the world contends that looking out for others, rather than self, results in ruin. For the Christian, however, looking out for others and standing steadfastly with them is essential to salvation—not the salvation of our eternal spirit, but our salvation from persecutors. Even as Jesus did not live in fear but in faith, we are to live in faith and trust God that, as we do things *His* way, He will protect us.

None of these three things that Paul admonished the church to do is easily accomplished! In fact, in our humanity, they are impossible. We must rely upon the Holy Spirit to help us discern the mind of Christ and choose to walk in obedience to the Lord. We must rely upon the Holy Spirit to help us yield to other people and love them, serving them as Christ served others. We must rely upon the Holy Spirit to help us overcome our fears related to those who seek to persecute us, thwart our efforts for good, or destroy us.

To what degree do you struggle to live in unity of mind and heart with other believers?

To what degree do you find it difficult to esteem others above yourself?

To what degree do you find yourself fearing the opinions of others, especially those who see your self-sacrificial behavior as being weak?

A
Application for Today

The eight-year-old boy slapped his paper from school on the desk in front of his father with the attitude of a conqueror. On the paper was a large red A+ and an added note, "Good work. 100%."

The father looked up at his son and then looked over the paper carefully. He enjoyed watching his son beam so broadly. Just a year before his son had been struggling in school. "Proud, aren't you?" Dad said with a grin.

"It's hard to be humble when you're perfect!" the boy said.

"Just make sure you don't get such a big head that it won't fit inside your baseball cap," Dad said.

The boy grinned, "I won't."

"I'm proud of you son," Dad said as his son left the room.

The father sat back in his chair and stared at the paper. *Good job*, he thought to himself. *Good thing we got that tutoring when we did. Good thing I made an effort to help with his homework. Good thing we built that study center upstairs.* Dad beamed.

"Good job, Dad," he finally said, aloud, not realizing that his wife had walked into the room behind him.

"You sound proud of yourself," she said.

He grinned as he said, "It's hard to be humble when you're the father of a perfect child."

Parents enjoy their children's achievements.

So does God the Father enjoy the achievements of His children.

What do you think delights your Heavenly Father the most about what you have done recently to give witness to Christ Jesus or to build up your fellow believers in their faith? Why do you think the Father delights in this?

S
Supplementary Scriptures to Consider

The apostle Paul regarded Jesus as being our greatest example of humility:

> Let this mind be in you which was also in Christ Jesus, who, being in the form of God, did not consider it robbery to be equal with God, but made Himself of no reputation, taking the form of a bondservant, and coming in the likeness of men. And being found in appearance as a man, He humbled Himself and became obedient to the point of death, even the death of the cross. Therefore God also has highly exalted Him and given Him the name which is above every name, that at the name of Jesus every knee should bow, of those in heaven, and of those on earth, and of those under the earth, and that every tongue should confess that Jesus Christ is Lord, to the glory of God the Father (Philippians 2:5–11).

• Name some of the biggest problems that you, or others you love, are facing. (For example, cancer, AIDS, divorce, rebellious children, loss of job, death of spouse, depression or despair.) What does it mean to you that the name of Jesus is above anything else that can be named?

• Not everybody, or every thing, presently bows the knee to Jesus or confesses that Jesus Christ is Lord. What does it mean to you to have hope that this will one day be so?

• We are not required to do what Jesus did, nor can we do what He did in our finite humanity. We can however, have the "mind" of Christ in humbling ourselves before God and doing whatever God asks us to do. What is the Lord asking you to do that requires a humbling of yourself before Him?

The concept of caring mutually for one another is expressed from cover to cover in the Bible, beginning with the first two siblings:

> Then the LORD said to Cain, "Where is Abel your brother?"
> He said, "I do not know. Am I my brother's keeper?"

And He said, "What have you done? The voice of your
brother's blood cries out to Me from the ground"
(Genesis 4:9–10).

• Note that God did not say to Cain that he was his brother's keeper, but
rather, God asked Cain, "Where is Abel?" Do you know where those you
love "are" in their spiritual life? Are you concerned about their spiritual
state? In what ways *are* you to be your brother's keeper? Are we to be
every person's keeper, or only the keeper of a "brother"—someone whom
the Lord has put into relationship with us as a family member, friend, or
fellow believer?

• At the point of the conversation in Genesis cited above, Cain had already
killed Abel. Cain responded to God as if he could keep a secret from
God. Are there secrets about the way you feel toward other people, or
have acted toward other people, that you believe have gone unnoticed by
God? For whose benefit did God confront Cain with the question, "Where
is Abel?"

Paul expressed concern for two women in the Philippian church who seemed to have been at odds with each other:

> I implore Euodia and I implore Syntyche to be of the same mind in the Lord. And I urge you also, true companion, help these women who labored with me in the gospel, with Clement also, and the rest of my fellow workers, whose names are in the Book of Life (Philippians 4:2–3).

• In what ways are we to be peacemakers between members of our church who may be at odds with each other? What are the difficulties encountered any time a person gets between two disputing people? How should we go about our peacemaking efforts?

I
Introspection and Implications

1. To whom are you indebted for sharing the Gospel of Christ Jesus with you? To whom are you indebted for modeling a Christian life to you?

2. Jesus commanded that we love others *as* we love ourselves (See Matthew 22:39). Is it possible to esteem others before self if we do not first experience the love of God ? If so, in what ways? If not, why not?

3. How do you define the concept of being the "keeper" of another person? What limitations do we face in being the "keepers" of our brothers and sisters in Christ Jesus?

4. What should be our course of action when we find ourselves in disagreement with other believers when it comes to discerning the mind of Christ or deciding what actions our church should take?

C
Communicating the Good News

What message is conveyed to an unbeliever when that person sees Christians standing fast in one spirit, and with one mind striving together for the faith of the Gospel?

What message is conveyed to unbelievers when they see Christians looking out for one another, rather than pursuing their individual self interests?

LESSON #3

STAYING ON COURSE

Enemy: something or someone that harms or opposes what is beneficial and good

B
Bible Focus

> *Beware of dogs, beware of evil workers, beware of the*
> *mutilation! For we are the circumcision, who worship God in*
> *the Spirit, rejoice in Christ Jesus, and have no confidence in*
> *the flesh, though I also might have confidence in the flesh. If*
> *anyone else thinks he may have confidence in the flesh, I more*
> *so: circumcised the eighth day, of the stock of Israel, of the*
> *tribe of Benjamin, a Hebrew of the Hebrews; concerning the*
> *law, a Pharisee; concerning zeal, persecuting the church;*
> *concerning the righteousness which is in the law, blameless.*
>
> *But what things were gain to me, these I have counted loss*
> *for Christ . . . and count them as rubbish, that I may gain*
> *Christ, and be found in Him, not having my own righteous-*
> *ness, which is from the law, but that which is through faith in*
> *Christ, the righteousness which is from God by faith; that I*
> *may know Him and the power of His resurrection, and the*
> *fellowship of His sufferings, being conformed to His death, if,*
> *by any means, I may attain to the resurrection from the dead*
> *(Philippians 3:2–11).*

The Philippian church had encountered false teachers. Paul referred to them as "dogs," a term normally used by Jews to refer to Gentiles. The image is one of a person who is highly destructive—dogs in the ancient world were generally scavengers, not family pets. They roamed the streets, attacking if necessary, but generally seeking out garbage pits and weaker animals for their food.

Paul used this strong metaphor to describe Jewish legalists who insisted that the Philippian Gentile converts undergo the rite of circumcision as a sign of their Christianity. Paul regarded the efforts of these false teachers as mutilating to the Philippians spiritually, even more so than physically. He quickly pointed out that, as a circumcised Jew and as a man once held in extremely high regard by the Jewish community in Jerusalem, he should know if circumcision had any relationship to Christian faith. His answer was a strong "no." Circumcision meant *nothing*—it did not lead to salvation and it was not necessary to affirm salvation. In fact, Paul wrote, *nothing* about keeping the law and being zealous for the law had contributed in the least to his salvation or had helped him maintain his salvation. Rather, it was faith in Christ—and only faith in Christ—that had brought him into right relation-ship with God the Father.

In essence, Paul was declaring, "I know what *doesn't* work when it comes to receiving Christ and living in Him. And I know what *does* work. Faith is what works."

The reason for Paul's admonition was this: he desired that the Philippian believers stay the course and not become sidetracked by "tacked on" rituals and customs that might lead them away from pure faith in Christ.

Paul recognized ultimately that all of our extraneous, religious manmade trappings—from our self-serving attitudes to our self-made habits—must be set aside if we truly are to live fully in Christ Jesus. It is Christ's life that we are to live, not our own.

What are some of the rituals and customs that might sidetrack us today from simple belief, which is all that is necessary for salvation?

How do we guard against substituting symbols and rituals for a genuine relationship with Christ Jesus?

How can we tell when we have encountered a false teacher?

A
Application for Today

The story is told of a godly man who sought to read his Bible and pray every morning for an hour before he went about his other chores and responsibilities. He generally spent this time with the Lord in the privacy of his own bedroom before joining others in his family for breakfast. The man was faithful in this discipline, but sometimes found that he became sidetracked when his cat wandered into his room and began to purr loudly as it rubbed against his pant leg. The solution to this problem? He leashed the cat to one of the bedposts while he spent his time reading and praying.

The man's son witnessed this behavior of his father. He grew up admiring his father's devotion and as he became an adult and moved out on his own, he sought to copy his father's discipline. He bought a cat and tied it to the bedpost just as his father had done, and then spent a little time reading his Bible and praying—unless, of course, he was running late. On most days, he spent only a few minutes in his devotional time, but he never failed to leash the cat to the bedpost.

That man, in turn, had a son who also admired his father and sought to be just like him. When he became an adult, he purchased a cat and faithfully leashed it to the bedpost each morning as he was getting dressed and ready for the day. When his little boy asked him why he was doing that, he replied, "I'm not quite sure, but my father always leashed his cat to the bedpost and he was a good man who loved God. I think maybe tying the cat to the bedpost was part of his faith ritual. So, I tie the cat to the bedpost, too."

Is there something in your life that has no *real* spiritual meaning, but which you regularly do?

S
Supplementary Scriptures to Consider

The apostle Paul presented a description of those who are the "enemies of Christ:"

> Brethren, join in following my example, and note those who so walk, as you have us for a pattern. For many walk, of whom I have told you often, and now tell you even weeping, that they are the enemies of the cross of Christ: whose end is destruction, whose god is their belly, and whose glory is in their shame—who set their mind on earthly things (Philippians 3:17–1).

• Do you know anyone who is an "enemy of the cross of Christ"? How does that person behave? What choices does that person make that are ungodly? How do they display a wrong set of priorities?

• What does it mean for a person to set his mind "on earthly things"? How can a person go through a day without some concern for earthly things? Or, is the emphasis in Paul's admonition to be placed on "concern" rather than on "earthly"?

• How do you interpret the phrase "whose glory is in their shame"? Can you cite examples of this in your world today?

Paul admonished the Philippians to remain steadfast:

> My beloved and longed-for brethren, my joy and crown . . .
> stand fast in the Lord, beloved (Philippians 4:1).

• What does it mean to you to "stand fast in the Lord"? How do we do this as Christians? What is the balance between being teachable and flexible (especially when it comes to yielding to others and adopting new styles) and standing fast in truth?

I
Introspection and Implications

1. Why is it difficult to discern at times "what to keep" and "what to toss"—what is rubbish and what is of eternal value—especially when it comes to our religious rituals and traditions?

2. What is the value of religious rituals?

3. Have you ever encountered someone who told you that there was something "outward and visible" that you needed to do in order to be fully acceptable as a Christian?

4. Some church people require their members to dress in certain ways as a sign of their piety. How do you respond to the idea of a "Christian dress code"?

5. Respond to this statement: Symbolic behaviors are never the "real thing" but they sometimes are helpful in reminding us of eternal realities.

6. Is there anything that you have ever given up for Christ that you wished you hadn't?

C
Communicating the Good News

How would you respond to this question from a non Christian: "What do I have to change about my life in order to be a Christian?"

How might your answer be different if the person asking the question is a new convert to Christ Jesus? Would your answer be different if the person had been a Christian for several years?

LESSON #4

PRESSING TOWARD THE HIGH GOAL

Press: to exert steady, great, and persistent effort in order to "force" something to move or work

B
Bible Focus

> *Not that I have already attained, or am already perfected;*
> *but I press on, that I may lay hold of that for which Christ*
> *Jesus has also laid hold of me. Brethren, I do not count myself*
> *to have apprehended; but one thing I do, forgetting those*
> *things which are behind and reaching forward to those things*
> *which are ahead, I press toward the goal for the prize of the*
> *upward call of God in Christ Jesus.*
>
> *Therefore let us, as many as are mature, have this mind;*
> *and if in anything you think otherwise, God will reveal even*
> *this to you. Nevertheless, to the degree that we have already*
> *attained, let us walk by the same rule, let us be of the same*
> *mind (Philippians 3:12–16).*

Which direction are you looking—to the past, or to the future? This is the major question that the apostle Paul poses to the Philippians in this passage.

Note that Paul did not tell the Philippians to forget their past sins or failures. Certainly those were among the things worthy to be left behind. Their past lives as Gentiles had been tainted by evil behaviors and practices, ungodly relationships, and faulty beliefs that contributed to emotional and spiritual turmoil. Paul, however, did not limit the "forgetting" to those things that had been evil, miserable, or troublesome. He admonished the Philippians to forget *all* "things which are behind." This included their past glories—their highest achievements, their best moments, their winning games, their special honors and awards. Rather than dwell on any aspect of the past, positive or negative, the Philippians were challenged to reach "forward to those things which are ahead."

Why? Because the future held incredible things for them that were infinitely better than anything in their past!

Paul was absolutely confident that the future for all believers holds perfection, which might also be described as wholeness or completion. The future holds our resurrection, eternal life, and glories beyond description. It holds rewards that cannot be measured or valued, and wonderful experiences that defy human comprehension because they are beyond anything that our present-day senses can take in. Paul wrote that there are things that Christ Jesus has "laid hold" for us—in other words, He has already purchased them, acquired them, and holds them for us.

Furthermore, Paul admonished the Philippians to *press* forward to lay hold of those things that Christ had for them. There is nothing passive about this word "press." It refers to an active seeking, pursuing, stretching to reach for, or striving to attain. The image that is evoked is that of a person wanting something to the point that he is willing to do virtually anything to acquire it. The goal that Paul is pursuing is clearly stated: "the prize of the upward call of God *in Christ Jesus*." Paul is pursuing Christ-likeness! He wants to become more and more like Christ Jesus, his Savior and Lord. And he will let nothing stand in his way.

Do you really want to become more like Jesus? Do you want to feel what He felt, say what He said, do what He did, and experience what He experienced? Do you want to feel what He feels right now, say what He desires to be said, and do what He intends to be done?

Do you *really* want this?

Are you willing to cast aside everything else that you may want to make this your number-one priority in life?

The apostle Paul made no claim to having attained this prize. After years of living a godly life and doing everything to yield to the life-transforming power of the Holy Spirit within him, Paul still knew that there was *more of Christ* ahead for him.

No matter how long you have known Jesus as your Savior, and no matter how closely you have sought to walk with Him as your Lord—no matter how much you are presently relying upon the Holy Spirit to do His work in you and through you—there is still *more* that God has for you. You are not yet *fully* like Christ Jesus.

Do you really want to be more like Jesus?

A
Application for Today

The four-year-old boy picked up a stool, struggled to carry it through the screen door, and plunked it down next to the '57 Chevy parked in the family driveway. The hood of the car was up and his father was working on repairing the engine of the old car. The little boy got up on the stool and peered into the engine next to his dad. "Whatcha doing, son?" the father asked without looking up, popping his chewing gum but remaining intent on the project before him.

"Bein' like you," the boy said without hesitation, popping the chewing gum in his mouth and not looking at his father but rather, staring at the engine. The boy did not perceive that he was fixing the car, or even helping fix it. He did not ask for tools to wield, or ask what his father was doing or how he might help. He was just being with Dad and doing what Dad was doing, and that was all that mattered.

Jesus said to his disciples on one occasion, "I must work the works of Him who sent Me" (John 9:4). On another occasion He said, "If you had known Me, you would have known My Father also" (John 8:19). Jesus was just like His Father—they were one and the same. Jesus did only what He knew was His Father's will—His actions were a visible and tangible sign of the Father's invisible and intangible desires.

Are you like your parents in some ways?

In what ways are you growing to be like your heavenly Father?

S
Supplementary Scriptures to Consider

Paul wrote this about the future that he perceived for both himself and the Philippians:

> For our citizenship is in heaven, from which we also eagerly
> wait for the Savior, the Lord Jesus Christ, who will transform
> our lowly body that it may be conformed to His glorious body,
> according to the working by which He is able even to subdue
> all things to Himself (Philippians 3:20–21).

• Paul knew that he was bound for heaven one day, but his real delight was in "eagerly waiting for the Savior"! Paul was ready for the Lord to "subdue all things" to Himself. Those things no doubt included all of the remaining imperfections that Paul saw in his own life. What do you want Jesus to "subdue" in your life?

The New Testament also says this about our "pursuit" of the things of God:

> Let us lay aside every weight, and the sin which so easily
> ensnares us, and let us run with endurance the race that is set
> before us, looking unto Jesus, the author and finisher of our
> faith (Hebrews 12:1–2).

- What keeps us from being able to "press" toward the goal? What hinders our pressing forward to become more like Jesus?

- Do you perceive life to be a race that requires endurance more than speed? Where does that race lead? What might we do to develop greater endurance?

Paul wrote this to the church in Corinth:

> Do you not know that those who run in a race all run, but one receives the prize? Run in such a way that you may obtain it. And everyone who competes for the prize is temperate in all things. Now they do it to obtain a perishable crown, but we for an imperishable crown. Therefore I run thus: not with uncertainty. Thus I fight: not as one who beats the air. But I discipline my body and bring it into subjection, lest, when I have preached to others, I myself should become disqualified" (1 Corinthians 9:24–27).

- The Greek athletes who competed at the great festivals of the Olympic and Isthmian games spent long months in training for the games. If they failed to complete the prescribed training regimen, they were barred from the games. Paul contended that, in order to become like Christ and to fulfill His will in both becoming and doing all that Christ required, we must live disciplined lives that are focused on *winning* the prize, not just competing or coming in second. How focused are you in running your race to become more like Jesus?

• To discipline the "body" means more than the physical self, but also one's emotions, mind, and all fleshly impulses and desires. Are you a disciplined person? Why is discipline important if one is to become Christ-like? In what ways might you become more disciplined? How does a person go about developing greater discipline?

• Who determines the winner of the prize when it comes to running this race?

I
Introspection and Implications

1. Whom do you admire or respect the most? Whom do you aspire to be like?

2. What is the foremost goal that you desire to attain in your life?

3. What do the words "intention" or "focus" mean to you? How do these words relate to your Christian walk? In what ways does the Lord call us to great intention and focus for all we say and do?

4. In what ways do you find it difficult to leave your past behind you and press toward your future?

5. Do you have great confidence that your future in Christ Jesus will be better than even the best moments of your past? Why or why not?

C
Communicating the Good News

How important is the concept of a "new future" to a presentation of the Gospel to an unsaved person? How do you describe that new future to an unbeliever? What makes the new future both attainable and desirable?

In what ways does becoming more like Christ Jesus mean that we become more and more zealous about winning lost souls, helping others find healing and wholeness, and bringing deliverance to those in spiritual bondage? In what ways is our involvement in evangelism a means of measuring our Christ-likeness?

LESSON #5

RISING ABOVE ANXIETY

*Anxiety: nervous agitation, worry, intense
apprehension of a real or imagined fear*

B
Bible Focus

> *Rejoice in the Lord always. Again I will say, rejoice!*
> *Let your gentleness be known to all men. The Lord is at*
> *hand.*
> *Be anxious for nothing, but in everything by prayer and*
> *supplication, with thanksgiving, let your requests be made*
> *known to God; and the peace of God, which surpasses all*
> *understanding, will guard your hearts and minds through*
> *Christ Jesus (Philippians 4:4–7).*

Perhaps the number one cause of emotional and physical distress in our world can be boiled down to one word: stress. Stress has been linked to a wide variety of ailments, from emotional depression to mental illness, to marital difficulties and the breakdown of family life, to lack of productivity and quality performance on the job, to physical ailments from cardiovascular problems to digestive disorders.

We sometimes think, perhaps, that our lives are more stressful today than the lives of those in Bible times. The environments in which most of us live may be different than those of the first century or before, and therefore, the stress factors may have changed in nature. But the existence and amount of stress are probably no greater today than they have ever been. We struggle today just as people have always struggled to maintain our health, provide sufficient food, shelter, and clothing for ourselves and our families, raise healthy children, educate ourselves and our children, live up to our self-expectations and the expectations of those we love, protect ourselves from human enemies and natural disasters, and above all, live a life reconciled to our Creator.

The apostle Paul addressed this human condition of stress by prescribing a solution that had three parts:

• *Praise.* Frequent, ongoing praise produces joy and inner strength to withstand stress. We can never praise God too much! He is worthy of all praise. The wonder of praising God is that the Lord becomes elevated in our minds and hearts to the point that we see God as greater than any problem that we might encounter. As God looms larger and larger in our spirit, life's difficulties appear smaller and smaller. We have a growing confidence in God and a lessening fear or anxiety related to the circum-stances around us. Praise gives us a God-perspective on life, and from God's perspective, all things are always under His control.

- *Gentleness.* This means that we hold life "gently." We do not cling to others, grasp for things, or lash out in anger—all of which reflect a deep fear that things are not under control and we are in danger of losing something valuable. To hold life gently involves a recognition that all things are transitory. Those who deal gently with people and situations have learned how to take delight in the special moment, stop to smell the flowers, admire beauty and quality without feelings of covetousness or greed, feel thankful for the tender care shown by others, and take the time to treat others with courtesy and kindness. When we approach life with a gentle attitude, life tends to give back gentle rewards—greater appreciation for the small moments of genuine sharing and love, value for the small accomplishments and victories, and a warm glow from small compliments and words of recognition.

- *Prayers Voiced with Thanksgiving.* Just as with praise, we can never voice our thanksgiving to God too much. When we give thanks, we experience a change in our perspective. We begin to catch a glimpse of the countless ways in which God has helped us, provided for us, protected us, or shown His love to us in the past. We also see how God is helping, providing for, protecting, and loving us in the present. And therefore, we have greater confidence in anticipating the ways in which God has promised to help us and love us in the future. Our confidence grows that God is always with us. In this assurance, we can ask for what we need with the expectation that God desires to meet our earthly needs in a way that is for our eternal benefit. He is the Lord who promises everlasting life to those who believe in Jesus as their Savior, and an abundant life to all who abide in Christ.

When you feel anxious or stressed out, turn to the Lord. Voice your praise to the Lord for who He is. Give thanks to God for what He has done, is doing, and promises to do on your behalf—spiritually, physically, emotionally, and in your relationships. Hold life gently in your hands, neither expecting too much of yourself or others in any given time frame, and be willing to trust God in any situation that He allows you to experience.

The apostle Paul stated that, if we do these three things, stress subsides and life takes on proper perspective. The end result is God's peace, a peace that cannot be rationalized or acquired by any means other than our trust that God is God, and He is our loving Father who delights in always giving us His best.

Are you feeling anxious, worried, fearful, or overly stressed today?

Try the Bible prescription.

A
Application for Today

No matter what she had tried, the 36-year-old woman simply could not find a way to get a handle on her life. She was tired of cramming 30 hours of "things to do" into a 24-hour day. She was weary of feeling that she was always scrambling and constantly behind. She was exhausted from feeling under-appreciated and over-worked. She was bone weary of giving and giving, with little emotional input and woefully inadequate sleep, unhealthful nutrition, and virtually no laughter.

One day she hailed a cab outside her inner-city skyscraper office building, went to the airport, and with only her purse and briefcase in hand, she boarded a flight to a beautiful but remote area of the United States, rented a car, and began to drive. She didn't care which road she took or where it took her by nightfall. She stopped only long enough to purchase a few personal hygiene items and a couple bottles of water. She made a quick phone call to family members to tell them where she was and that she was taking a 48-hour break. And then she headed out, down a road that appeared on the map to have two lanes and lots of curves.

Within ten miles, she was slowly making her way along a river through dense, sun-splattered woods with mountains rising on both sides of the narrow valley. She began to pray, "Lord, help me. I don't know how to make sense of my life." Clearly she heard deep within her spirit, "Follow My road. Listen to Me."

She replied, "Lord, I am following the best I know how. I'm listening to You the best I know how to listen. But where am I going? Why am I so overwhelmed?"

Again, she heard deep within her spirit, "Look at the road." She looked at the road that unfolded ahead of her. She could see only the next hundred yards or so before the road curved to the right and was hidden by the dense foliage, but the area around her was beautiful and the pavement smooth. She saw no other car on the two-lane road—it was as if this road and this pristine and serene environment had been created just for her. She suddenly realized, "I am on God's road in my life. I cannot see too far ahead, but what He reveals is beautiful all around me. I need to enjoy the journey."

She said aloud, "You are the road, aren't You, Lord?" A great peace engulfed her. She slowed the car a little to take in even more of the scenery. Peace flooded her soul. She began to sing soft praises to the Lord.

"I love it here, Lord," she said. "But what about when I get back to the city?"

"Follow My road. Listen to Me," were the words that she heard again in her spirit.

In an instant, she knew that, if she spent time with the Lord as her first priority each morning, He would set her on the path to experience and do what *He* desired, and that what *He* wanted to be done in any given day would be sufficient. She perceived that a beautiful individualized path would unfold before her day by day, even through the dense "forest" of city skyscrapers and bustling days.

And so it was.

What road are you traveling today?

Are you on the Lord's road?

Are you doing only what *He* requires of you? Or are you attempting to do all sorts of things that you require of yourself, or others seem to require of you?

Are you listening to His wise counsel before making your plans?

Are you voicing praise and thanksgiving to Him at every turn of the road?

S
Supplementary Scriptures to Consider

Paul said this to others in the early church about praise and thanksgiving:

> Rejoice always, pray without ceasing, in everything give
> thanks; for this is the will of God in Christ Jesus for you
> (1 Thessalonians 5:16–18).

• How is it possible to "rejoice always?" In what ways can praise to God become our first response to everything that happens in life? In what ways can praise become the attitude or mind set that we have toward life?

- How is it possible to "pray without ceasing"? In what ways can we live with an ongoing total reliance upon God for direction, provision, and protection?

- How is it possible to give thanks to God "in everything"? In what ways does the voicing of thanks and appreciation change our attitude and make us more aware of God's abiding presence?

The psalmist gives one of the greatest antidotes for anxiety in the Bible:

> Thus my heart was grieved,
> And I was vexed in my mind.
> I was so foolish and ignorant;
> I was like a beast before You.
> Nevertheless I am continually with You:
> You hold me by my right hand.
> You will guide me with Your counsel,
> And afterward receive me to glory.
> Whom have I in heaven but You?
> And there is none upon earth that I desire besides You.
> My flesh and my heart fail;
> But God is the strength of my heart and my portion forever.
> (Psalm 73:21–25)

- Try closing your eyes and visualizing the Lord taking you by your right hand and walking with you through your day. What could possibly harm you with the Lord by your side?

The psalmist gives us deep insight into the nature of thanksgiving. Read these two passages:

1) We give thanks to You, O God, we give thanks!
   For Your wondrous works declare that Your name is near. (Psalm 75:1)

2) It is good to give thanks to the LORD,
   To declare Your lovingkindness in the morning,
   And Your faithfulness every night." (Psalm 92, 1–2)

- These verses from Psalms admonish us to give thanks for all of the "wondrous works" of God. Can we ever reach the end in identifying all his wondrous works? Why is it important to count our blessings and name them aloud to the Lord?

- The psalmist tells us to praise God for His love in the morning and thank Him for His faithfulness every night. How might framing our days with praise and thanksgiving change our attitude toward other people and circumstances that we encounter? How does reminding ourselves of

God's love and faithfulness change our perspective on the difficulties that we may encounter?

Paul wrote this to the Colossians:

> Continue earnestly in prayer, being vigilant in it with thanksgiving (Colossians 4:2).

• What does it mean to you to be "vigilant" in praying with thanksgiving?

Certainly one of the most "soothing" psalms for those who feel anxiety is Psalm 91. Memorize it!

> He who dwells in the secret place of the Most high
> Shall abide under the shadow of the Almighty.
> I will say of the LORD, "He is my refuge and my fortress;
> My God, in Him I will trust."
> Surely He shall deliver you from the snare of the fowler
> And from the perilous pestilence.
> He shall cover you with His feathers,
> And under His wings you shall take refuge;
> His truth shall be your shield and buckler.
> You shall not be afraid of the terror by night,
> Nor of the arrow that flies by day,
> Nor of the pestilence that walks in darkness,
> Nor of the destruction that lays waste at noonday.

A thousand may fall at your side,
And ten thousand at your right hand;
But it shall not come near you.
Only with your eyes shall you look,
And see the reward of the wicked.
Because you have made the Lord, who is my refuge,
Even the Most high, your dwelling place,
No evil shall befall you,
Nor shall any plague come near your dwelling;
For He shall give his angels charge over you,
To keep you in all your ways.
In their hands they shall bear you up,
Lest you dash your foot against a stone.
You shall tread upon the lion and the cobra,
The young lion and the serpent you shall trample underfoot.
"Because he has set his love upon Me, therefore I will
          deliver him.
I will set him on high, because he has known My name.
He shall call upon Me, and I will answer him;
I will be with him in trouble;
I will deliver him and honor him.
With long life I will satisfy him,
And show him My salvation (Psalm 91).

• Reread this psalm aloud and circle the words and phrases that stand out in a special way to you. What is the Lord speaking to your heart?

The essence of joy is praise, and praise focuses on the unchanging nature of God. The psalmist called the people of God to exalt the Lord for His many attributes. Read these two verses:

1) "Praise the Lord!
   O give thanks to the Lord, for He is good!
   For His mercy endures for ever." (Psalm 106:1)

2) I will sing praises to You among the nations,
   For Your mercy is great above the heavens,
   And Your truth reaches to the clouds (Psalm 108:4).

- Three of the foremost things for which we can praise God are His good-
  ness, His mercy, and His truth. Identify several aspects of each of these
  attributes of God for which you personally give praise:
  GOODNESS—
  MERCY—
  TRUTH—

The Lord hears all of our prayers. The psalmist gives us an important key,
however, to what must always be at the center of our prayers: an awareness
that God is faithful and righteous, and that he desires to protect us from our
enemies, teach us to do His will, and to lead us in the way that we should
walk—a way of uprightness:

> "Hear my prayer, O LORD,
>   Give ear to my supplications!
>   In Your faithfulness answer me,
>   And in Your righteousness. . . .
>   Cause me to know the way in which I should walk.,
>   For I lift up my soul to You.
>   Deliver me, O LORD, from my enemies;
>   In You I take shelter.
>   Teach me to do Your will,
>   For you are my God;
>   Your Spirit is good.
>   Lead me in the land of uprightness (Psalm 143:1, 8–10).

• Note that the psalmist specifically asks for three things: for God to lead him into the right path for him to walk, for deliverance from his enemies, and for instruction on those things that are God's will. In what specific ways are you seeking these three things in your life:

LIFE DIRECTION (PERHAPS DAILY DIRECTION)—

DELIVERANCE FROM ENEMIES—

KNOWING GOD'S PLAN AND PURPOSES—

I
Introspection and Implications

1. How much of your prayer life do you devote to thanksgiving and praise? Do you feel a need to make any adjustments in the way that you pray, give thanks, or offer praise to God? If so, how will you go about making those adjustments?

2. Do you hold life gently? Do you treat others with gentleness? If not, how might you have a more "gentle" approach to your life? What will be the advantages?

3. How does thanksgiving give you confidence that God can meet your needs, and even desires to meet them?

4. How does praise give you assurance that God can take control over your circumstances, and already is in charge of all things?

5. In what ways are fears, worries, anxieties, or feelings of being stressed-out contradictory to faith? In what ways do our fears and anxieties keep us from taking risks with our faith?

C
Communicating the Good News

How do the things that make us "stressed out" keep us from doing the will of God?

Do you ever miss opportunities to share the Gospel with another person because you are too intent on maintaining your schedule or accomplishing your agenda? What changes might you make?

LESSON #6

THE GODLY THOUGHT LIFE

*Meditate: to reflect upon, to contemplate
calmly, seriously, and at length*

B
Bible Focus

> *Finally, brethren, whatever things are true, whatever things are noble, whatever things are just, whatever things are pure, whatever things are lovely, whatever things are of good report, if there is any virtue and if there is anything praiseworthy— meditate on these things. The things which you learned and received and heard and saw in me, these do, and the God of peace will be with you (Philippians 4:8–9).*

What do you think about?

It is important to know what we think about, fantasize about, and imagine, because it is our thought life—including our beliefs, values, and attitudes— that give rise to what we say and what we do. As the writer of Proverbs noted: "As he thinks in his heart, so is he" (Proverbs 23:7). What we think about becomes the pattern from which we cut the fabric of our days.

Paul admonished the Philippians to take charge of their thought lives and to focus on things that are:

TRUE—things in agreement with the eternal truths evident in God's Word and creation; lasting and permanent concepts and principles, not transient philosophies, daydreams, manmade theories, or speculations.

NOBLE—things that give honor and value to life.

JUST—things in harmony with the absolutes of right and wrong established in God's Word, and the principles of God's justice (which is always replete with mercy and offers of forgiveness, as well as with consequences for all human behavior).

PURE—those things associated with chaste, honest, and innocent living; things that are above reproach and that produce holiness.

LOVELY—things that give delight and innocent pleasure to oneself and to others; things that are experienced as blessings.

GOOD REPORT—things that all people agree are virtuous and that produce mutually beneficial results for all involved.

We are to think about those things that build us up in character, promote our faith, and create in us a healthy and generous respect for ourselves and others.

Paul also provided a perspective toward evaluating all of life: "If there is any virtue and if there is anything praiseworthy." In other words, Paul was saying, "Look for the good. Look for the silver lining. Believe the best in others, rather than the worst."

Finally, Paul told *how* to think: "meditate on these things." To meditate is to mentally rehearse, to repeat continually, and in the process, to create a mindset or to memorize. What we think about often enough becomes a mental habit. It is our mental habits that dictate our behaviors. In other words, the Philippians were to *focus and concentrate* on these things. If we concentrate on what is true, we will speak what is true. If we focus on what is noble, just, and pure, we will act in noble, just, and pure ways. If we pursue thoughts that are lovely and of good report, we will live in a way that others perceive to be lovely and worthy of praise.

Paul, however, did not limit himself to what and how the Philippians were to think. He also told them to *do* what they had learned, received, heard, and seen. They were to *act* on the Word that Paul had taught them, the salvation and gift of the Spirit which they had received, the Gospel that Paul had preached, and the example of daily Christian living that Paul had modeled before them as he lived among them and worked alongside them.

We learn not only from books and media reports, but from life itself. Perhaps most importantly, we learn from people—from what they tell us and even more so by the way in which they carry out their daily responsibilities and choices. Choose to seek out the best possible learning experiences and books, and then implement what you learn. Choose to learn from the best Christians you know, and then copy their example!

When our thoughts are godly, and our actions accurately display our godly thinking, we experience a peace within. We have integrity—a total match-up of our inner and outer behavior. We experience greater wholeness.

We also have greater feelings of peace with God. Why? Because Paul actually described in this passage the way that God thinks and the way that God reveals himself to us! God's thoughts are 100 percent true, noble, just, pure, lovely, and of good report *all the time*. Contrary to many people's perception that God is on the look-out for sin in our lives, God is always searching for what is virtuous and praiseworthy in us. God is continually seeking to teach us how to be in the best position to receive His blessings, pouring out His goodness toward us, speaking to us of His love and tender care, and revealing Himself to us in ways that produce in us genuine joy.

What are *you* thinking about today?

What is *your* perspective on life?

How did you acquire that perspective?

From whom are you learning how to live in Christ Jesus?

A
Application for Today

The woman rose early and, after a morning jog along the main shopping street of her neighborhood—where she encountered numerous billboards and shop displays—she returned home to prepare for her day, all the while listening to morning news reports on both radio and television. Most of the news was about tragedies and disasters, plus the death of a popular figure in the entertainment world. The banter among the morning talk-show hosts was mostly speculative as they conjectured about what might happen next, who would do what, who might be held accountable, and what might have caused the famous person's death.

The commute to work was a bombardment of more advertisements and slogans, for everything from abortion clinics to pain relievers to divorce attorneys. At work, she encountered co-workers who were quick to share the tragedies of their lives, including the infidelities of their friends, the illnesses of their parents, the bad behavior of their children at school, and their spouse's indifference or angry rages. Their monologs were punctuated with four-letter words.

Her work as a research assistant for a political lobbyist led her to an eight-hour confrontation of statistics about the current opinions of society and the character profiles of her elected officials—the overall picture was not particularly encouraging or moral. In an attempt to escape the onslaught of negative opinion and facts, she closed her office door and watched a soap opera during her lunch hour. The plotline dealt with relationships mired in dishonesty, poor communication, sexual dalliances, and greed. The alternatives, she sighed, were an interview program that probed the depths of human degradation, or more news. The soap opera seemed the least of three evils.

Back at home, after a commute of more billboards and an hour listening to the evening news—with more reports of death, disaster, and dastardly deeds—she sat down with her husband to watch television. The comedy hour had more sexual innuendos and jokes than she could count. The drama hour had more violence in one 20 minute segment than she had ever personally witnessed in her entire life. She and her husband discussed watching a movie, but it offered only more overt sexual behavior and violence, plus degrading language. They opted to turn off the television and read. The novel that she had started seemed to present only more of the same messages that she had encountered all day—she admitted that she could hardly expect more from a murder mystery.

She finally went to her bedroom at ten o'clock and curled up in her bed with her Bible, thinking that she would read something positive for a few minutes before going to sleep. Five minutes of Bible reading later, she was snoring soundly, glasses still on her face and her bedside light still on.

The woman gave this daily report to her spiritual advisor after she had told her advisor that she couldn't seem to shake general feelings of apprehension and fear in her life. Her advisor had asked her to give an hour-by-hour rundown of the messages that she was taking into her life. After listening to the report given above, the advisor asked simply: "Are you telling me that you believe five minutes of faith-building truth can comfort you and overturn nearly 17 hours of images and messages that promote life-destroying sin?"

It was the only question that the advisor needed to ask. The next day, the woman dramatically revamped her daily schedule and the types of sensory "input" that she welcomed into her mind.

If someone asked you to give a daily run-down of the messages that you take in to your life—visual, aural, and sensory—what would your hour-by-hour report include?

S
Supplementary Scriptures to Consider

The psalmist knew that all things "praiseworthy" were to be found in the nature and manifested works of God through the ages:

> I cried out to God with my voice. . . .
> In the day of my trouble I sought the Lord . . .
> And I said, "This is my anguish;
> But I will remember the works of the LORD;
> Surely I will remember Your wonders of old.
> I will also meditate on all Your work,
> And talk of Your deeds.
> Your way, O God, is in the sanctuary;
> Who is so great a God as our God?
> You are the God who does wonders;
> You have declared Your strength among the peoples.
> You have with Your arm redeemed Your people
> (Psalm 77:1–3, 10–15).

• What do you personally believe to be the most awesome works of the Lord?

• What do you believe to be the "wonders" of God?

• In what ways do you perceive that God has declared His strength before the people of the entire world?

• In what specific ways has God provided for the redemption of His people?

• How does recalling the awesome, wonderful, and redemptive works of God change our attitudes? Build our faith?

• How do you personally "meditate" on God's works? What is it that might be learned from a close examination of virtually any creature, natural process, or natural law? What is it that can be learned from a study of history—not only about human nature, but about God's sovereign plans and purposes?

• What is the benefit of openly talking about God's deeds? Who is the number-one audience for what we say? How does voicing God's deeds build up faith inside us?

• What does it mean to you to feel "anguish"? Why is it important when we feel turmoil to remind ourselves about the works of God?

I
Introspection and Implications

1. Reflect on your own thought life and behavior in the last six months. How has it influenced your choices and decisions? How has it influenced your actions?

2. How do we best teach our children to focus their thoughts on what is true, noble, just, pure, lovely, and of good report? Do we do our children a disservice by keeping them from many of the world's messages and images? Why not? If so, in what way?

3. Many people report that, when they choose to turn off the negative messages of the media, they have a sense of withdrawal or isolation. Have you ever experienced this? What did you do? What was the ultimate result?

4. In what ways is the Lord challenging you to reevaluate your daily schedule and the types of sensory input that you take into your mind?

5. How carefully do you evaluate your sources of information?

6. How carefully do you *choose* those that you allow to teach you, or to model behavior for you? In what areas might you make better choices?

7. How do you discern what is worthy of study? Of remembering? Of forgetting?

8. When was the last time you memorized something that you believed to be true, noble, or praiseworthy in content? What might you choose to memorize next?

C
Communicating the Good News

What is the role of giving an unsaved person something "good" to think about—even if it is just one good idea or quote?

One of the great benefits of memorizing portions of Scripture is that a person has *at all times* something to think about that is true, noble, just, pure, lovely, or of good report. A second great benefit is that we always have something that is virtuous to say to an unbeliever. A third benefit is that we always have something that is praiseworthy to say to a fellow believer. Which passages of the Bible do you think are the most important for you to memorize? What tips might you share with another person about the best way to memorize Scripture? To use Scripture in conversations with unbelievers? To use Scripture to edify fellow church members?

LESSON #7

THE KEY TO CONFIDENCE

*Confidence: belief in and assurance of
a final successful outcome*

B
Bible Focus

> *I rejoiced in the Lord greatly that now at last your care for me has flourished again; though you surely did care, but you lacked opportunity. Not that I speak in regard to need, for I have learned in whatever state I am, to be content: I know how to be abased, and I know how to abound. Everywhere and in all things, I have learned both to be full and to be hungry, both to abound and to suffer need. I can do all things through Christ who strengthens me.*
>
> *Nevertheless you have done well that you shared in my distress. Now you Philippians know also that in the beginning of the gospel, when I departed from Macedonia, no church shared with me concerning giving and receiving but you only. For even in Thessalonica you sent aid once and again for my necessities. Not that I seek the gift, but I seek the fruit that abounds to your account. Indeed I have all and abound. I am full, having received from Epaphroditus the things sent from you, a sweet-smelling aroma, an acceptable sacrifice, well pleasing to God. And my God shall supply all your need according to His riches in glory by Christ Jesus. Now to our God and Father be glory forever and ever. Amen (Philippians 4:10–20).*

Paul had lived at the top of life—enjoying the best and finest that various cultures had to offer. He had also been in circumstances too terrible for most people to comprehend. He had experienced mountain-top spiritual adventures, and he also knew what it meant to be alone, misunderstood, abandoned, and suffering. He had known the "high" of personal popularity, and the "low" of rejection and persecution. He had come to this conclusion: circumstances don't really matter. What happens, happens—and no matter what occurs, it is only temporary. Even if a situation lasts a hundred years, it is only temporary. Furthermore, Paul knew that everything that transpires is under God's control. God allows circumstances to take place and He uses them to work in us, or through us, something that will be for eternal good.

Our role is not to look at our circumstances but to turn to the God who controls our circumstances.

Our hope does not lie in a reversal of circumstances, but in the One who transcends every situation.

Our part is not to wallow in circumstances, but to look for the lessons and the victory that God has for us as we live through our circumstances.

What was important to Paul was not the environment or difficult situations that we might face in our lives, but the way in which we *regard* life's occurrences. Paul wanted the Philippians to adopt his attitudes of contentment and confidence.

Contentment did not mean that Paul *liked* negative experiences. He was writing from prison, and would have preferred to be free. He had experienced lack, and was grateful for provision. Rather, Paul's contentment rested in the fact that, no matter how terrible his situation might be, he could find a way to speak the Gospel within that circumstance, and in so doing, give eternal meaning and purpose to whatever was happening in his life.

It is as we find a way of proclaiming the goodness of God, the love of Christ, and the power of the Spirit in any environment, that the environment becomes transformed into a holy sanctuary.

It is as we present the Gospel or praise God in a place or time, that we give eternal meaning to that moment, experience, or encounter.

It is as we bring the name of Jesus into a conversation that we create a holy moment for God to do eternal work in our life and the life of the person with whom we are conversing.

Paul's confidence was not rooted in his personal ability to endure hardship. Rather, his confidence was in Christ—He knew that it was Christ who gave him the ability not only to survive but to thrive in any situation. His confidence rested in the truth that Christ could supply from His eternal riches all that was *necessary* to live another day with joy and to give another message for the sake of eternity.

Are you abasing or abounding today?

Does it matter, with regard to your attitude?

Are you fully using the situation in which you find yourself as a platform for presenting Christ Jesus to others?

A
Application for Today

The man hardly knew what to do first. His wallet had been lifted from his back pocket while he was standing on the platform of a European subway, and although he had given chase to the thief, he now found himself standing on the sidewalk above the subway station—alone, winded, and without any means of proving who he was or paying for even a cab ride back to his hotel. His money, his passport, his credit cards, and even the name and address of his hotel had all been tucked into the wallet. He didn't speak the language of the nation that he was visiting, and he wasn't sure where his friends had gone for the afternoon or how he might reach them even if he knew where they were. He had never felt as alone as he did in that moment.

He began to walk in the direction of his hotel, trying to remember the names of streets that he had seen on a map earlier that morning. Before he walked very far, he paused to look closely at a street sign, and perhaps in response to the look of puzzlement on his face, a passerby asked if he needed help. The man who stopped spoke English and the robbed man jumped at the opportunity to tell his story and ask for advice. The helpful man did more than give advice. He offered to accompany him back to his hotel, and once there, he helped him explain his problem to the hotel concierge, who did not understand English very well. The benefactor then offered to take the man to the local American Express office to cancel his credit card and to obtain replacement traveler's checks. He dialed the US Embassy on his behalf and as a parting gesture of good will, gave him the equivalency of $20 in cash. He spent more than two hours providing all the help that he could give.

"I don't know how to thank you," the robbed man said. "Please give me your business card so I can repay you when I get back to the United States."

The man replied, "You can repay me best by helping someone else in need."

The American thought for a moment and then, feeling a surge of inspiration, asked softly, "You are a Christian, aren't you?"

The helpful man's face brightened. "I am. Are you?"

Suddenly the entire afternoon took on a new dimension. The two men shared their faith over a cup of coffee and the next evening, the American went to have dinner with his benefactor's family in their home. There they had further opportunity to share their faith and give praise to God. Before the evening ended, they had forged a friendship that lasted for many years. Out of their friendship they established a joint business venture for publishing Christian curriculum and Gospel literature.

The Bible tells us repeatedly that what the devil means for our harm, God turns to our good. Have you experienced this in your life?

S
Supplementary Scriptures to Consider

It has been said that your faith can grow only to the degree that you perceive God to be infinitely great—powerful, wise, and loving in His sovereignty over all things. The psalmist said this:

> The LORD is gracious and full of compassion,
> Slow to anger and great in mercy.
> The LORD is good to all,
> And His tender mercies are over all His works.

All Your works shall praise You, O LORD,
And Your saints shall bless You.
They shall speak of the glory of Your kingdom,
And talk of Your power,
To make known to the sons of men His mighty acts,
And the glorious majesty of His kingdom.
Your kingdom is an everlasting kingdom,
And Your dominion endures throughout all generations.
The LORD upholds all who fall,
And raises up all who are bowed down.
The eyes of all look expectantly to You,
And You give them their food in due season.
You open Your hand and satisfy the desire of every living
    thing.
The Lord is righteous in all His ways,
Gracious in All His works (Psalm 145:8–17).

• In what ways have you experienced God's graciousness? His compassion?

• In what ways have you experienced God being slow to anger?

- In what ways have you experienced God's tender mercies?

- How would you describe the "majesty" of God's kingdom?

- What are examples of God's "dominion" enduring throughout all generations?

- In what ways have you experienced the Lord upholding you when you have fallen? How has he raised you up when you were bowed down?

• Why do we look expectantly to the Lord to provide *all* that we need, and not look to other people to meet our needs? What are some of the needs that only God can meet?

• Cite ways in which the Lord has opened His hand and satisfied your desires?

I
Introspection and Implications

1. When have you been "abased"? When have you "abounded"? How do you look back on those circumstances? Did your circumstance or the environment in which you found yourself affect your attitude? In what ways does attitude influence a circumstance or environment?

2. Have you learned in whatever state you find yourself to be content? Is this difficult for you? How so?

3. Are you in a situation or environment today that is less than desirable? What might you do to feel greater contentment?

4. Reflect upon Paul's statement: "I can do all things through Christ who strengthens me" (Philippians 4:19). Do you fully agree with that statement? Cite practical examples in your life in which Christ strengthened you in areas where you were weak.

LESSON 7 • The Key to Confidence **85**

5. Have you ever accomplished more than you thought you could in a particular arena of work? In what ways did Christ enable you?

6. Paul wrote that he was happy to receive the gift that had been brought to him in prison, not only because it filled a need in his life, but because he believed in "the fruit" that would abound to their account. In other words, Paul was expecting God to honor their gift with an abundance of supply to meet *their* needs. Have you ever experienced this—in giving something to another person, needs in your life have been met in unusual, divine ways? How did this happen?

7. Paul wrote these words of encouragement to the Philippians: "My God shall supply all your need according to His riches in glory by Christ Jesus" (Philippians 4:13). What does it mean for us to have *all* our need supplied? What does this phrase mean to you: "the riches in glory by Christ Jesus"? What is at Christ's disposal to give to us? How does Christ's presence ultimately meet all our needs?

C
Communicating the Good News

So many people have a negative impression of God as a harsh and mean-spirited judge. How important is it in our evangelistic efforts to present the love and tender mercies of God to those who do not know Jesus as their Savior?

Have you ever had an experience in which simply introducing the name of Jesus into a conversation or situation made a difference? What happened?

Many people live in a situation of need, a feeling of discontentment, or a state of feeling unworthy and weak. What hope would you offer to such a person from this passage in Philippians? What is the impact of believing that Christ wants to meet our needs, give us contentment, and help us in every area of our life?

How does Paul's phrase, "I can do all things through Christ who strengthens me" relate to any hesitation or weakness that you feel when it comes to sharing the good news of Jesus as Savior?

NOTES TO LEADERS
OF SMALL GROUPS

As the leader of a small discussion group, think of yourself as a facilitator with three main roles:

- Get the discussion started

- Involve every person in the group

- Encourage an open, candid discussion that remains Bible focused

You certainly don't need to be the person with all the answers! In truth, much of your role is to be a person who asks questions:

- What really impacted you most in this lesson?

- Was there a particular part of the lesson, or a question, that you found troubling?

- Was there a particular part of the lesson that you found encouraging or insightful?

- Was there a particular part of the lesson that you'd like to explore further?

Express to the group at the outset of your study that your goal as a group is to gain new insights into God's Word—this is not the forum for defending a point of doctrine or a theological opinion. Stay focused on what God's Word says and means. The purpose of the study is also to share insights on how to apply God's Word to everyday life. *Every* person in the group can and should contribute—the collective wisdom that flows from Bible-focused discussion is often rich and deep.

Seek to create an environment in which every member of the group feels free to ask questions of other members in order to gain greater understanding. Encourage the group members to voice their appreciation to one another for new insights gained, and to be supportive of one another personally. Take the lead in doing this. Genuinely appreciate and value the contributions made by each person.

You may want to begin each study by having one or more members of the group read through the section provided under "Bible Focus." Ask the group specifically if it desires to discuss any of the questions under the "Application" section . . . the "Supplemental Scriptures" section . . . and the "Implications" and "Communicating the Gospel" section. You do not need to bring closure—or come to a definitive conclusion or consensus—about any one question asked in this study. Rather, encourage your group that if the group does not *have* a satisfactory Bible-based answer to a question that the group engage in further "asking . . . seeking . . . and knocking" strategies to discover the answers! Remember the words of Jesus: "Ask, and it will be given to you, seek, and you will find; knock, and it will be opened to you. For everyone who asks receives, and he who seeks finds, and to him who knocks it will be opened" (Matthew 7:7–8).

Finally, open and close your study with prayer. Ask the Holy Spirit, whom Jesus called the Spirit of Truth, to guide your discussion and to reveal what is of eternal benefit to you individually and as a group. As you close your study, ask the Holy Spirit to seal to your remembrance what you have read and studied, and to show you ways in the upcoming days, weeks, and months *how* to apply what you have studied to your daily life and relationships.

General Themes for the Lessons

Each lesson in this study has one or more core themes. Continually pull the group back to these themes. You can do this by asking simple questions, such as, "How does that related to _____?" . . . "How does that help us better understand the concept of _____?" . . . "In what ways does that help us apply the principle of _____?"

A summary of general themes or concepts in each lesson is provided below:

Lesson #1
JOY THAT CHRIST IS PREACHED
Integrity in a believer's life
The two-fold witness of our words and our life

The human need for recognition and applause

Confronting our own motives in Christian witness and service

Being a faithful and bold witness

Lesson #2
UNITY THROUGH HUMILITY

Living in agreement with other believers

Esteeming other believers "better than ourselves"

Living without fear of our enemies

Humility—yielding to God and respecting others

Christ's example of humility

What it means to be the "keeper" of any other person

Being our brother's "keeper"

Lesson #3
STAYING ON COURSE

Rituals and customs that enhance faith

Rituals and customs that detract from faith

Accurate discernment of false teachers and false teaching

Dealing with the enemies of the cross of Christ

Lesson #4
PRESSING TOWARD THE HIGH GOAL

The balance between remembering the past and dwelling in the past

The balance between hoping for the future and dwelling in the future

Pursuing the perfection of Christ Jesus

Hindrances to our pursuit of Christ-likeness

Maintaining a focused and intentional Christian life

Lesson #5
RISING ABOVE ANXIETY

The role of praise in dealing with anxiety, stress, or fear

The role of thanksgiving and prayer in dealing with anxiety, stress, and fear

The role of holding life "gently" and treating others in gentleness in dealing with anxiety, stress, and fear

Establishing a consistent, ongoing discipline of prayer, praise, and thanksgiving

Ways of developing "gentleness" as a virtue in our lives

Lesson #6

THE GODLY THOUGHT LIFE

Taking control of one's thought life

Developing a godly perspective on all people and situations

Learning how to live the Christian life from godly mentors

Meditating upon and memorizing Scripture

Lesson #7

THE KEY TO CONFIDENCE

Contentment regardless of circumstances

Trusting God to supply all your needs

Feeling confidence in Christ's ever-present help

Introducing Jesus into every environment, every situation, and every relationship that we
encounter

NOTES

NOTES

NOTES

NOTES